Sugar Gliders

The Ultimate Pet Owner's Manual on All You Need to Know about Sugar Gliders, How to Care for Sugar Gliders & Where to Buy or Adopt a Sugar Glider

Jeanette R. Gibson

Copyright© 2016 by Jeanette R. Gibson

Sugar Gliders

Copyright© 2016 Jeanette R. Gibson
All Rights Reserved.

Warning: The unauthorized reproduction or distribution of this copyrighted work is illegal. No part of this book may be scanned, uploaded or distributed via internet or other means, electronic or print without the author's permission. Criminal copyright infringement without monetary gain is investigated by the FBI and is punishable by up to 5 years in federal prison and a fine of $250,000. (http://www.fbi.gov/ipr/). Please purchase only authorized electronic or print editions and do not participate in or encourage the electronic piracy of copyrighted material.

Publisher: Enlightened Publishing

ISBN-13: 978-1530144365

ISBN-10: 1530144361

Disclaimer

The Publisher has strived to be as accurate and complete as possible in the creation of this book. While all attempts have been made to verify information provided in this publication, the Publisher assumes no responsibility for errors, omissions, or contrary interpretation of the subject matter herein. Any perceived slights of specific persons, peoples, or organizations are unintentional.

This book is not intended for use as a source of legal, business, accounting or financial advice. All readers are advised to seek services of competent professionals in the legal, business, accounting, and finance fields.

The information in this book is not intended or implied to be a substitute for professional medical advice, diagnosis or treatment. All content contained in this book is for general information purposes only. Always consult your healthcare provider before carrying on any health program.

Table of Contents

Chapter 1: Sugar Glider Basics 3
- Physical Characteristics 4
- Breeding 6
- Other Facts 8

Chapter 2: Buying a Sugar Glider 11
- Things to Consider before You Buy 11
- Questions to Ask before You Buy 14
- Buying Sugar Gliders off the Internet 19
- Do I Have to Buy More Than One? 21
- Male or Female? 24
- Finding Support 25
- Is It Really Possible to Adopt Sugar Gliders? 26

Chapter 3: Make a Home for Your Sugar Gliders 29
- Building a cage 29
- Placement of the Cage 35

Interior Decoration 36
Things for Them to Play with 38
Food Dishes 39
Safety First 40
First Introductions 41
Glider-Proofing Your Home 43

Chapter 4: Caring for Your Sugar Gliders 51
What is Your Glider Trying to Say? 51
Potty Training 54
Bonding 57
General Care 59
How Do You Know If Your Pet Is Sick? ... 62

Chapter 5: Feeding Your Sugar Gliders 65
Recipe of Homemade Diet 70
Treats 72
Foods to Avoid 73

Conclusion 75

Chapter 1: Sugar Glider Basics

Congratulations on taking your first step towards owning a sugar glider! This book will help answer questions you may have about purchasing your new pet. We will discuss sugar glider basics, and also touch on topics such as things to consider before buying your new pet and things he or she will need in order to be comfortable in their new home.

First we will go over some sugar glider background. Sugar gliders are originally from Australia, New Guinea, and their surrounding islands, particularly in forests that have a good supply of eucalyptus, acacia, and gum trees. They are nocturnal; during the day they sleep in their nests and become very active and engaging after sundown.

The Latin name for the sugar glider is *Petaurus breviceps*, and it is a species of marsupial. It is also sometimes called a "sugar bear" because they can stand up and make very loud noises in order to scare away possible predators. It gets the common name "sugar glider" because it enjoys eating fruits and it is also capable of gliding through the air through base jumping techniques, which is essentially hopping from fixed objects and gliding between them. Sugar gliders can glide up to 45 meters, and while in flight they can manipulate their paths so that they can even catch bugs in their mouth before landing.

Physical Characteristics

Sugar gliders have soft, fuzzy, squirrel-like bodies. Females are slightly smaller than the males, but their length from the nose to the tip of their tails is about 24 to 30 centimeters, or 12 to 13 inches. Without the tail, their bodies are 5 or 6 inches long. They have soft, thick fur coats that are generally bluish-grey but can sometimes be tan or yellow. They also generally have a black stripe from about halfway up their back to the tip of their nose, and the belly, throat and chest are also generally a light cream or white color.

Sugar gliders are very vocal and communicative creatures. They produce a variety of sounds, such as chirping, barking, chattering, and crabbing. While all sugar glider owners hear these noises coming from their pets, there are also several others that people find difficult to describe.

A fun fact about sugar gliders (among many!) is that they have prehensile tails, which means that they can hold and grasp objects with their tail. A prehensile tail helps the sugar gliders climb and pick up objects, but it also helps them to balance. Because of the amazing balance provided by their tails, sugar gliders can suspend themselves at incredible angles. They cannot however hang from their tails, because the tail is only partially prehensile and very, very delicate to the touch (because of this you should make it clear to small children that it is not a handle for the glider and should not be grabbed!). They even use the tail as a rudder while in flight, and sometimes curl it around them as a cloak to stay warm.

Sugar gliders' hands and feet have opposable thumbs and four fingers, with fingers and toes sharp as hooks, which help them grasp onto tough surfaces. The feet are unusual because the second and third fingers are fused together and helps the sugar glider groom itself, and also from the fifth finger along the side of the body and connecting to the first toe is something called the patagium; it is the membrane that extends when the legs are stretched out that allows the mammal to glide through the air, and runs along the whole length of each side of the body.

Because a sugar glider is a marsupial, it also has a couple of characteristics that it shares with its cousins, the much larger kangaroo and the koala bear! Female gliders have a pouch on their bellies. Their babies live in these pouches for two and half months after birth.

One final important physical characteristic about sugar gliders is that they have scent glands on their forehead, chest, and cloaca (the opening at the bottom of the intestinal, reproductive, and urinary tract). On males, you can see the gland on their foreheads because there is a bald spot there. This is one of the ways to tell a male from a female.

Breeding

In the wild, sugar gliders generally have a territory of about 1,000 square meters as long as there are plenty of places to be used as shelter. Sugar gliders use hollows up high in trees to build their nests, and can live in groups of up to 8 adult gliders and the current young. The dominant male in the group marks the others with his scent and saliva, which helps him identify intruders who are not part of the group and expel them from the nest. The hollows are lined with leaves.

Females can have one or two babies at a time, and the gestation period only lasts 15 to 17 days, after which the baby or babies will crawl into the pouch to develop further. It is very difficult to tell that a female is pregnant until the baby is in the pouch and growing, which makes the pouch look lumpy and extend from the body.

The baby will stay in the pouch for up to 70 days, eventually spilling out. The mother can become pregnant again while she still has joeys in her pouch, but she is remarkably capable of suspending the pregnancy until her pouch is empty.

It takes approximately two months before the joey is weaned from the mother and they are independent at four months of age. In captivity, a female is capable of breeding multiple times a year because of consistent diets. Males reach sexual maturity starting at 4 months of age, and females can be sexually mature starting at 8 months.

It is important to note than having a sugar glider is a long-term commitment; they can live for up to 12 years in captivity.

Other Facts

While sugar gliders can be very active and energetic, they do sometimes experience a condition known as torpor. This happens in cold weather, drought conditions, and rainy nights due to a lack of food. Sugar gliders need a varied and extensive diet because it uses a lot of energy, so when there isn't a lot of food available it can enter into torpor for anywhere between 2 and 23 hours a day and rest.

You will be able to notice that by a reduction in activity levels and a regular bodily temperature, which helps it to avoid torpor for longer through saving energy. Torpor is an emergency measure that happens for sugar gliders in the wild more often than it will happen to your pet, but it is good to be aware of the condition so that you can keep an eye out for it.

The sugar glider is not an endangered species. It is very adaptable and capable of living in difficult environments, which is good because of the reduction of its natural habitat in Australia in the past century. It is, however, illegal to own a sugar glider in Southern Australia without a permit, and you cannot capture or sell them there without a license that is generally only issued for research purposes.

Outside of Southern Australia, sugar gliders are very popular pets, although it is one of the most common animals to be found in the illegal pet trade because they are taken from their natural habitats (don't worry, this guide will help offer suggestions for finding reputable places to purchase them as they are bred in large numbers in the United States, among other places). Not all American states allow them as pets, including California, Hawaii, Alaska, Pennsylvania, and Massachusetts.

Now that we have discussed some basic physical characteristics of sugar gliders and a little about their background, we will move into some more of the fun stuff (and the important stuff, too) that you should know before choosing to make one a new member of your family. First we will talk about the buying process, and then we will move into care requirements including how to construct a suitable cage, what to feed it, and answering basic questions about potty training and bonding.

Chapter 2: Buying a Sugar Glider

As I already mentioned, buying a sugar glider is a long-term commitment. Also, because sugar gliders bond deeply with their owners, it is one you must take seriously and with full knowledge of what the potential responsibilities will be so as to not harm yourself or your sugar glider further down the road. This chapter will help clarify some things you should consider before choosing a sugar glider as a pet, will help you find options for purchasing one, and will answer many questions you may have.

Things to Consider before You Buy

First, let's go through some things to consider about what differentiates sugar gliders from other pets and what some of the perks and responsibilities come along with ownership. Sugar gliders can be great little friends, but like all animals, they aren't for everyone.

Sugar gliders are incredibly loyal, playful, and affectionate. They really, really love your attention! They will be happy just sitting in your pocket and sleeping all day, since they are nocturnal and won't be incredibly active for much of the day. Unfortunately, this means that the owner (you) needs to be able to play with them and spend time with them every day.

The more time you take to get to know them and to sit with them, the better your relationship and the healthier your sugar glider will be. If you leave them along too long, they can easily become ill and depressed. But really, spending time with them shouldn't be difficult, because they do enjoy just curling up in your lap or in a pocket and napping. This is one of the most important facts to consider because they absolutely thrive on your love.

That being said, sugar gliders are surprisingly low-maintenance! They rarely bite, unless they are a baby or a poorly trained adult. They can't be technically trained to use a litter box, but they are clean and predictable and there are certain potty-training techniques you can use in training. However, you should be prepared for the possibility of a cage that needs frequent cleaning and also the possibility of your glider having a bowl movement while they are playing with you or climbing on you.

Creating a healthy and balanced diet only costs about $10 a month, and in that regard they are much cheaper than your ordinary house cat or dog—also, unlike those larger mammals, gliders never need vaccines or heartworm medications or anything like that. They also don't smell any worse than a puppy when they are properly fed (diet is something we will cover later on in this book) but some people do find their smell irritating, because they will on occasion mark their territories with a special scent.

Sugar gliders can also be a little noisy— because they are nocturnal, it is probably best to not keep their cage in the room where you sleep. They also can hiss or bark to communicate. All of these factors should be taken into consideration before you make a commitment to a sugar glider and then realize you have to give it up for adoption.

While feeding a glider per month is on the low end in comparison with some other types of pets, cost is certainly something to take into consideration when you purchase a new pet, especially one with as long a lifespan as a sugar glider.

You should generally expect to pay between $200 and $400 for a healthy 8 to 12 week old baby. If a deal sounds like a price that is too amazing to be true, you should probably walk away from it. You should never buy a discounted glider from the internet or from a rescue where you can't meet the people selling it to you in person.

So, aside from a pricey initial startup cost, gliders become relatively cheap little friends. There aren't many hidden expenses and caring for them becomes pretty simple, and barring health emergencies that require veterinary appointments (and when this happens the bill is still going to much, much less than that for a cat or dog), you will only be paying the monthly cost of food.

Questions to Ask before You Buy

Now that you know some of the things you should consider when deciding whether or not a sugar glider is the right companion for you, we'll go through a list that I have adapted from the Association of Sugar Glider Veterinarians with 7 questions you should ask before you buy a new sugar glider from what you think may be a responsible breeder:

Does the person selling you your sugar glider have a valid and current USDA license?

Breeding sugar gliders is strictly regulated at the federal level, and it is not like buying a new kitten or puppy. In fact, in some states you are required to provide proof that your sugar glider was purchased directly from a USDA licensed facility. The rules the USDA has set in place for breeding operations are there for the safety and welfare of the animals, and you should NEVER believe anyone who says that a USDA license is not important. If someone says that to you, you should not buy from their breeding establishment.

Can you hold some of their adult animals?

No reputable breeder will be OK with strangers handling the baby sugar gliders, but it should be fine for you to interact with the adults. This is good, because the way adult animals interact with you is a good way to judge the breeders. If the animals are all friendly and easy to handle, you know that the establishment knows what they are doing. Also, the gliders should not be restrained in any way. Well-trained sugar gliders like their owners and bond very easily, so they would not be on a leash or zipped away where you can't see them. So definitely make sure that the adults are well behaved and well cared for, and if the seller won't let you see them for some reason you should walk away.

While you are interacting with the animals, make sure you ask the seller a lot of questions about their surroundings and just to be sure that the seller sound professional and caring. If they seem disinterested or confused and lacking confidence in the answers they are giving you, you should be hesitant to proceed with the transaction.

What kind of support do they offer after the sale?

Reputable dealers go to a great deal of trouble to keep in contact after the sale has been made. Many even provide lots of formal education programs for their buyers with written material and online instructional videos to help with spur of the moment questions. There should also be a way for you to contact them with questions or emergencies.

Does your sugar glider come with a health guarantee?

You should try to have your sugar glider inspected by a qualified veterinarian before you adopt it, and a reliable breeder will not take issue with that procedure or with giving you a health guarantee. Standard industry policy is a 2 to 3 day replacement policy, should the baby unexpectedly die, and sometimes it is possible to have that extended to a week to 10 days. The Association points out that if there is anything seriously wrong with the baby, it won't live longer than a day or two, so this is actually a good policy even though 2 to 3 days may not seem like a long warranty period.

How old are the babies when they are adopted?

The ideal age for bonding is between 8 and 12 weeks out of the pouch. A good way for you to tell if it is old enough is that the glider's tail should be bushy, instead of slicked down or flattened.

Are the males already neutered, or will that be an extra fee?

Males should be neutered as soon as possible, and a veterinarian's office can charge between $75 and $150 for the operation. Most reputable breeding facilities already have their males neutered before you get them, and don't charge extra for it. But you should definitely double check just in case.

How and when will you receive your new baby?

It is extremely rare that you can go in for a sugar glider and leave with one on the spot. This is because sugar gliders breed fairly slowly and they are in high demand, so many times you will order your baby, pay, and then wait a few weeks for the call (another reason to make sure you are dealing only with a licensed dealer, so you know the process is legitimate). Don't let them be shipped to you in an airplane or anything like that—the health risks are too great! And the transportation is difficult for the glider. Driving will be fine.

Buying Sugar Gliders off the Internet

We have already briefly touched on the subject of avoiding dealings with breeders on the internet, but this is a subject that it is important you be fully educated on because there is a lot of misinformation online in order to get people to spend money wastefully and also to discredit reputable breeders and practices. In general, it is very unsafe to operate on information found solely online, and you should research good resources to use when you can't reach your breeders, veterinarians, or other experienced members of the sugar glider community for advice.

One of the biggest ways you can be harmed by relying on the internet is by buying a discounted glider or by believing everything you read about reputable breeders that you find online. The best way to examine a breeding facility is to go there in person, and online breeders will purposefully spread lies about good breeders in order to sell more gliders. This is unsafe, and contributing to this illegal activity (which it will be, because few online retailers will actually be USDA certified) is only going to prolong the suffering of sugar gliders in that industry. Always meet your seller in person.

Another way that internet advice can damage you and your glider is that not everyone knows the best way to feed a sugar glider, but lots of people THINK that they know! Amateur blogs and videos are filled with poor advice about feeding your baby. Poor dietary practices are what cause most of the issues seen in veterinary offices today.

In general, although websites may look legitimate and promise to promote the welfare of gliders, they are actually touting outdated diets and practices, and illegally traffic sugar gliders.

Some good resources for you can be found at the North American Sugar Glider Association, or www.mynasda.org, and at the Association of Sugar Glider Veterinarians, www.asgv.org. Otherwise, there are lots of good books in print, and again, face-to-face communication is great so you know it is coming from an experienced source.

Do I Have to Buy More Than One?

Another common question people have about buying their first sugar gliders is whether or not their glider will be OK without a second glider as a friend. There are a lot of pros and cons involved here, so we'll go through what will happen in either situation and you can make your own educated decision on what you think will be best for your situation, both in your personal life and the amount of time you have to devote, and also financially.

It is generally assumed that a sugar glider will die from loneliness without another sugar glider to play with, and this simply isn't true. They can get lonely, absolutely, but as we discussed earlier in the chapter, this is why it is important that you know you can spend time with it and show it affection, because it is very playful and loving and will not do well if left entirely on its own (again, don't panic about this requirement! They love to just chill out with you, nothing strenuous is necessary).

The reason they get lonely is because they generally live in groups of anywhere from 6 to 15 other animals, and so they are incredibly social by nature. Studies have proved that gliders can get bored and even suffer from clinical depression when they are a solitary glider with little to no interaction with their owners.

This can be avoided by spending a couple hours a day with your gliders, and most people follow that guideline and only own one glider as a household pet. They typically do just fine in these scenarios.

Of course, if you ARE going to buy two, you should do it early on so they can bond together. Older gliders will need to be "introduced" with much more patience and time, in separate cages that are nearby each other at first for a week or so for them to get to know each other a bit (we will discuss this more in later chapters). Then, it will be necessary to watch them closely to make sure they are getting along alright.

If you do want to only get one and are worried about it becoming depressed, here are some signs you can watch out for:

- Lack of appetite

- Inactivity at night when they are generally much more active

- Excessive fur-pulling, self-mutilation, or licking

- Possibly excessive barking (although the ASGV suggests lots of reasons are possible for barking)

Really though, if you are able to spend a couple of hours a day or more you're your glider, just by having them in your pocket or near you, and spend as much time with them as you can, they will be just fine.

Also, to keep them from being bored you should supply a large cage and fun toys, pouches, branches and other objects to fill it with for them to stay occupied and interested in their surroundings (we will touch on cages further along in the book. You can also inquire with your breeder if they have a "second baby discount," which is often standard.

So, while two may be ideal, one will be OK too as long as you are observant and willing to give a lot of affection to what will be a very loyal and loving companion. It is up to you to decide what will be best for you and your glider, either way you decide to go, and it's no one else's decision.

Male or Female?

People oftentimes have difficulty choosing between a male and a female. There isn't a big difference in size—males are only slightly larger—but there are a couple of other notable differences you should take into consideration that mostly deal with physiology. Males have a bald spot on the top of their heads where there is a scent gland, but once they are neutered those generally fill in. Females have a pouch on their tummies where they keep their young.

But as far as personality differences, it really comes down to the owner. Some people say males can be more aggressive, and some people say females can be more aggressive. What it comes down to is how you treat your animal and bond with it, and the time you take to train it. If you don't take any time with it, it isn't going to be sweet to you, no matter the gender. There is no real reason to go for a male over a female, or vice versa. Each sugar glider, like any pet, has a distinct personality.

Finding Support

Finally, a really great way to figure out if a sugar glider is right for you is to talk to someone who currently owns one. They will be able to tell you more than you could learn from the internet or from someone who is trying to sell you one, because they are just a regular person like you who made a leap and decided to incorporate one into their family. Breeders are knowledgeable but they are also very passionate, and speaking instead to another person who started out in your shoes could be really beneficial to you in this process.

Keep in mind that occasional visits to the veterinary office will happen. Because of this, you should double check with the vets in your area to see if any of them specialize in exotic pets. Otherwise, you could buy a sugar glider and find out you do not have a very stable support system for him or her in case of an emergency, especially if the breeder you bought it from is far away or offered little support post-purchase.

Is It Really Possible to Adopt Sugar Gliders?

In this chapter, we have talked about places to buy a sugar glider, but one more option that is important to shed light on is the possibility of rescuing a sugar glider. Unfortunately, many people think that they want to buy a glider and then after a few days or weeks decide that it was a mistake, and these animals are abandoned.

However, there are good and bad ways to go about rescuing an animals. First, as mentioned before, you should avoid all dealings online. Some legitimate looking websites exist out there but the truth of the matter is there is no way to know for sure who you are dealing with or the type of animal you are getting, and generally these "organizations" are just scams. But, if you think that adoption is the right path for you, here are a few things you can do.

First, the Association of Sugar Glider Veterinarians operates a network on the national scale where people can offer up their gliders for adoption or legally adopt one of their own through connections with your local veterinarian. They have to be members of the network, but signing up is free and once they are involved they can participate in the adoptions for their customers, and be notified when a glider becomes available. All adoptions are free and the animals are given a health checkup before being handed over to you.

The second thing you can try is to call the animal shelters near your home and ask about the frequency of sugar glider cases. They can put you on a list to be notified if one ever becomes available.

Please know that these two adoption scenarios are very rare. But, if you feel strongly about rescuing an animal instead of going through a breeder, you do have these options available to you.

Chapter 3: Make a Home for Your Sugar Gliders

Once you have decided that a sugar glider is the pet for you and you have decided how to go about finding one, either through a breeder or an adoption, it is time to start preparing to welcome it into your life. In this chapter we will discuss how to get ready for your new baby; we will talk about setting up its cage, introducing it to other pets and people, and common household dangers for sugar gliders.

Building a cage

Before you bring it home, you need to make sure it will have a warm and safe place to sleep! Sugar gliders are unusual pets in that they need pretty large cages so that they have lots of room to jump around, and it is important that the cages have a good vertical height as well so that they can climb. A general guideline for two sugar gliders is 2'x2'x3', so it is taller than it is wide or long.

Most of the cages you can buy from a pet store or online are not quite large or tall enough, so in order to provide maximum comfort many owners create their own cages. They do this with wire mesh and melded wire. You should be sure that the mesh on the cage is not so large that the glider can escape, but is also wide enough so that it can climb. Generally, spacing between the mesh should be no more than 1/2 an inch to one inch.

I will provide a set of instructions below, but be advised that if you do not like these specifications there are plenty of variations available on the internet; these are just general guidelines for a basic cage that is 2'x2' x 3' (this cage is very tall with several platforms—this way, the sugar glider can have lots of exercise in order to promote good health, and there is plenty of space for toys and creative play which can help it develop mentally as well).

Note: These instructions were adapted from the website "Sugar Gliders and Other Exotic Pets" at http://www.angelfire.com/tx/facehugger/index. html.

You will need the following items:

- 18 feet of 24" wide 16 gauge vinyl PVC coated wire mesh with spacing that is no larger than one inch, and no smaller than 1/2 inch (it is important that the mesh be coated so that the gliders will not cut their delicate feet when climbing. Also, if there is not a good coating then when it starts to chip off your glider could be exposed to toxins)

- 200 cable ties (they come in packs of 100) or J clips (also called cage clips) and J clip pliers

- 2 separate lengths of 8 foot plastic trim

- Wire cutters

- Pliers

- Hot glue or silicone sealant

- Door latch

Assembly Instructions:

1. Cut the 18 feet of wire mesh into the following sections: 1 piece of 12 inch by 2 foot mesh (this will make up the door), 2 sections of 6 inch by 2 foot pieces (these will be the shelves), 2 sections of 2 foot by 2 foot pieces (this will be the top and bottom), 4 sections of 3 foot by 2 foot pieces (this will create the sides).

2. Cut a hole 22 inch tall and 10 inch wide in the center of one of the 3 foot by 2 foot sections—this will be the opening for the door.

3. Attach one length of plastic trim on three sides of the door and on the inside edges of the opening (leave the side you attach bare).

4. Using J clips or cable ties to secure the door 1 inch from the edge of the hole. The door should overlap the hole on all sides by 1 inch. Then attach the door latch on the other side.

5. Lay the four 3 foot by 2 foot pieces (including the one you just cut into) side by side

in a row on the floor, making sure that the one that has the door you just made has the door latch facing the floor.

6. Attach the long edge of each shelf to the sides of the cage where you want them to go.

7. Glue the plastic trim to the edge that will be facing out when you are done.

8. Attach one edge of the top of the cage to one of the sides.

9. Attach the bottom in the same manner, except you raise it an inch or two so that the bottom of the cage will ultimately be above the bedding (preventing disease later on).

10. Note: If you want a sliding tray, raise the bottom high enough to accommodate the tray and remove the extra wire on only one edge of the bottom to help keep it in place.

11. If you do not do a sliding tray, you will leave the excess wire and then place the whole cage in a large tray—it is better that the tray exceed the size of the cage by a couple of inches on each side to catch anything such as bedding, food, or excrement

that has fallen from the main body of the cage (this will help keep your house/carpet much cleaner than it would be otherwise).

12. Attach the sides with the cable ties or J clips, and finish adding ties to the top and bottom.

You should now have something that looks like a sugar glider cage! Try to lift it up and move it around a little bit to make sure it is secured and safe, and add cable ties or J clips where necessary. If you used silicone sealant instead of hot glue, you should wait 24 hours prior to placing the sugar glider into the cage to make sure the silicone is set.

The most important part of the cage, once you know that the mesh is too small for them to escape, is being incredibly sure that the latch for the door is secure. Sugar gliders are very intelligent and can learn to open their cages, and sometimes can get loose. This is especially true at night when they are most active, and most likely to get bored.

The bedding for your cage should consist of a layer of aspen or fir shavings, but cedar shavings could negatively affect your glider. This will help absorb waste, and depending on the number of gliders you own should be cleaned at least once or twice a week. When rinsing the tray under the cage after you have removed the bedding, many people recommend using a mixture of baking soda and water helps with odor control a great deal. Also, if you have a male, be careful not to overdo it. Cleaning a male's cage too frequently could cause them to mark their territory with their scent glands more often, which will make it smellier than it was before.

Placement of the Cage

The cage should not be placed in direct sunlight and should also avoid drafts, because sugar gliders are sensitive to extreme temperature changes. Ideal temperatures for a sugar glider range from 75 to 80 degree Fahrenheit. You can help them maintain steady body temperature by providing them with things like heat lamps or heat rocks that have nesting cloths by them, so that if they get cold they can snuggle up next to a heat source.

Also, consider the placement of the cage in terms of what room it will be in—bear in mind that gliders are most active at night, and maybe you will want to have it a little bit away from your bedroom. The other place to avoid is the kitchen, because of all the fumes and cleaning solutions that are present. If you put it in an active and social place, like the living room, it will be much easier to spend lots of time with them since they will always have people around.

Interior Decoration

Now that we have built the new home for your little friend, it is time to think about interior decoration! There are many things you can provide for your glider in order to help it feel happy, healthy and safe.

Because sugar gliders enjoy curling up in small, dark places, you should provide a nest box. These can be bought from pet supply stores, or you can fashion one on your own. Some recommended possibilities for next boxes include unglazed clay pots that have holes in the sides (like many planters), and wood.

You can also use plastic nest boxes. The advantage to a plastic box is that they can be more easily cleaned that those made of clay pots or wood, which have a tendency to absorb odors and urine. Because of this, nest boxes made from clay or wood need to be replaced on occasion. The nest box should be placed towards the top of the cage, ideally against the ceiling.

Alternatively, you can use a pouch made of soft cloth, and affix the pouch to the side of the cage using cable ties or any other method. Cloth pouches are nice because they are washable and can get very clean. An added bonus of the cloth pouch is that if you use a carabineer or another method of attachment that can be easily removed it can help with bonding to your sugar glider, because once it is in the pouch you can just remove the pouch and take it with you without aggravating your new glider.

Unless you are using a cloth pouch, do provide bedding material (but not wood, so the glider won't eat it) in the nest box for added comfort and ease in cleaning. Also, be sure that whatever it is can be easily removed through the door of the cage.

Things for Them to Play with

Because sugar gliders have lots of energy at night, when you are asleep, you should provide them many toys to play with to keep them from getting bored and also to make sure they are physically healthy. Fresh branches are a nice touch, but high maintenance. If you want to use fresh branches for them to climb on, be sure that they don't have pesticides or fertilizers on them and are not from a coniferous tree (all of these things are toxic to gliders). Coniferous trees are types like pines and cedar, because they produce a sticky sap. Other good climbing toys are ropes and ladders.

Wooden toys generally made for birds and rodents are great for gliders. Cloth toys are not so good, because they can produce loose threads. When you are spacing these out, try to place them towards the top of the cage, because that is where your babies will spend most of their time.

An exercise wheel can also be incorporated for exercise if you have young gliders who can become accustomed to using it—you should use a larger one with a solid, plastic surface so that their tail does not get caught, and people do make wheels specifically for sugar gliders.

Also, it is not unusual to let your glider roam around in a plastic ball much like pet hamsters do. You can find these balls in any pet supply shop. Another great technique is to insert a length of PVC pipe. The gliders can run along it and use it for playing and hiding.

A more unconventional toy idea comes from the ASGV, who recommend taking a piece of nylon rope and tying it in knots, then dangling it from the center of the cage. The gliders will go nuts for it, and when you wake up in the morning you will be surprised to see that some of the knots have been untangled (like I mentioned earlier, they are very smart creatures!)

Food Dishes

Don't forget one of the most important additions when furnishing a new home for your pet—food dishes! The ones that are made for birdcages that can hang on the sides of cages are great, because they are out of the way. You want them to be big enough for the glider to access, but not so big that they can sit in them.

If you want to use a water bottle be sure to train your gliders to use it—otherwise, provide another dish with water in it.

Safety First

For safety reasons, be sure that nothing you put in the cage can be eaten (unless it is meant to be eaten) or choked on. Avoid loose strings or wires, and be sure that the toy can be washed. Keep in mind that they play a lot at night when you will be trying to sleep, so if you give them something with a bell you may want to remind yourself at night to take the bells out. Also, if you just got your sugar glider you should limit the number of toys you give it in the cage at first. If there are too many distractions for it you will have a harder time bonding.

When all is said and done, the ultimate goal of the cage is to reduce stress and anxiety for your sugar glider. For a baby glider, start them out in one of these basic cage sizes, and as it gets older if you would like to increase the size of the cage then go for it, especially if you have more than one. But in the meantime, when they are young it is easier for them to play and leap about without fear of falling. If they don't feel confident that they are safe in their cage when playing they can become less active. You can help them feel safe by providing plenty to climb on and hold onto, and lots of soft places to sleep and hide.

As always, avoid purchasing a cage online unless you are sure it is made of quality materials. This will avoid health problems later on.

First Introductions

Many people on the internet will tell you that it is impossible for sugar gliders to get along with other animals, but that is simply not true. With a lot of patience and love, you should be able to get sugar gliders to acclimate to your other pets just fine (provided your other pets want to be friends, too!). This is mainly because, as I mentioned in the introduction, sugar gliders naturally live in colonies. They like to bond with groups and families, and it is one of the reasons they like to have so much attention from humans.

It is the easiest to achieve this bonding when they are between 8 and 12 weeks out of their mother's pouch. I would recommend not leaving them alone with cats, at least at first, until you know how the cat will react. This is because many cats are conditioned to eating small rodents, not cuddling with them (ever seen Tom and Jerry?).

The best way to approach integrating your sugar glider into the lives of your other pets is to do it slowly. Start off by taking pieces of cloth and rubbing one on the glider and one on your other animal, and then give the cloth to the other pet. By doing this you are allowing the animals to get used to the scent of each other without the risk of a physical encounter. You should do this for a few days, at least.

Next, with the other animal is on a leash, introduce them to the glider while the glider is still safe in its cage. Do this slowly as well, and while using all precaution you think is necessary. Sugar gliders are naturally dominant species, and when confronted with another animal their first instinct will be to act like a tough guy, standing on its back legs and making small charges at the other animal as a protective instinct. Allow this to happen, safely.

After steps 1 and 2, you can begin to allow the other animal to smell the glider through your hands or a bonding pouch, and then using your best judgment and the knowledge you have of your animals and their personalities take it from there.

Gliders will typically bond will with many of the more traditional house pets, like cats and dogs. Birds can be more difficult, and so can small rodents, as sugar gliders have a natural fear of large birds and they tend to prey on small rodents in the wild.

Do try to keep them away from the less traditional house pets, such as snakes, spiders, and reptiles—these animals rarely get along with sugar gliders and it is best that they be kept apart.

Always remember that the more slowly the better. There is no rush to get your animals introduced and you shouldn't risk anything by trying to hurry the process along. Also, it could be in the end that maybe your new glider and your other pets aren't going to be best friends. That is ok, as long as they can live under the same roof.

Glider-Proofing Your Home

Just like toddlers, sugar gliders can be very mischievous and get into lots of trouble when you aren't paying attention and they are loose in your house. Just as you would baby proof your home when you bring home a new child from the hospital, you should take some steps to make sure that your house is safe for the new glider. Once gliders have bonded with you and are tame there is no reason not to let them play and exercise, as long as they are doing so in a safe space.

To begin, I would like to point out that a great option sometimes is to let the glider play in a tent. Perhaps you have one glider-proof room, but would like to bring the glider with you into the living room as well, which hasn't gotten as much attention yet in terms of making it safe. Well, if you set up a child's play tent and put some toys in there, it is a great option for a play pen. Also, this way you don't need to worry about the glider running off, crawling into an air vent, or being picked up and manhandled by a child or other pet. If it is big enough you can even sit in there with it!

One of the most common cases of accidental deaths with sugar gliders is drowning. This can happen with any pool of liquid, but is frequent with open toilet lids, sinks, bathtubs, buckets, swimming pools, or pots of liquid on countertops. You can avoid an accidental drowning by making sure doors are closed and putting lids on everything before you let the gliders out to play during the day. Sugar gliders cannot swim, at all, so don't even try it.

Another common form of injury and/or death is exposure to toxins. Sugar gliders are incredibly curious and have a powerful sense of smell so they are drawn to sweets easily, such as scented candles, air fresheners, and household cleaners (especially the ones that smell like citrus). Avoid this by making sure all of these types of objects are put away or behind closed doors before playing with the glider outside of the cage.

Other sources of toxins and dangers are insect and rodent traps/poisons, pesticides from foods and those sprayed around the house. Because of this, always wash their fruits and vegetables carefully before you feed them, remove the cage from the house to another house if you are going to have insecticides sprayed in your home, and don't leave dead bugs or rodents that have been killed by pesticide around the house.

Sugar gliders can also be exposed to toxins from drinking tap water in some areas (which will introduce them to chlorine and fluoride), and also from licking your hands. So many things come into contact with your hands during the course of the day, so always wash up before playing with the glider. If it licks them, it could be ingesting things like gasoline, cleaners, bug spray, sun tan lotion, etc.

Also, gliders can't eat everything you can eat. Never give them chocolate, for example. The meals you cook in your kitchen also may not be glider-friendly, due to all the hot things that can burn them and the smells that will draw out their curious nature. Because of this, keep the gliders in their cage when you are cooking.

These are just some of the big things you can do to get your home prepared. Always use common sense, too. Keep in mind that not every room needs to be 100% glider proof, because sugar gliders don't need to have free rein over your whole house. If you do one room, that should be good enough for them to play around in, and then if you walk around with them in your pockets the rest of the time they should be fine as long as you don't forget they are with you (like when you are cooking).

In case you are still worried after doing the above that things aren't safe enough, here are some other basic things you can check:

- Be sure all window screens are secure and don't have holes.

- Be careful with soft, fluffy furniture as gliders can get in between the cushions and get crushed when you sit down.

- Plug your drains—you wouldn't want to find the glider in your garbage disposal (this goes along with being aware of them when they are in your kitchen, or just not letting them in there at all).

- Cover all the outlets with outlet plugs, and check plugs and cords in outlets to make sure they aren't being pulled out or chewed on—secure all loose cords.

- Remove anything you don't want them to mark or spray urine on, like computer equipment.

- Keep the ceiling fan off.

- No hot surfaces, like portable heaters.

- Medications and over the counter drugs like Tylenol should be out of reach.

- Check the distance between the bottom of the door and the floor—if you can fit your finger between it, they can probably squeeze under it, and you should plug it with a towel, rag, or t-shirt.

- Cover fish tanks.

- Somehow block access to air conditioning and heating vents.

- Make sure there are no holes into your walls or ceilings that they can access, and you should make sure there are no openings into baseboards or appliances—gliders can fit into areas with an opening the size of your finger.

- Don't use your stove if you can't find your glider, because they can crawl down through the coils (unless if you have a closed off stove top, like a flat electric range)

- Watch out for your other pets, just to exercise caution.

- Latch the door behind you when you leave the glider-safe room so that they cannot get out.

- Make sure fireplace is closed off—it is easy for them to crawl up the bricks in the chimney.

- Remove household plants, except those that aren't dangerous to sugar gliders, especially if you do not want them sprayed or chewed on.

When you wake up in the morning you should always know where your gliders are, in case they got out of their cage and their room during the night. If you do not know where they are, don't sit on anything or turn on the stove. Also, don't sleep with them! They can get between the covers and be crushed if you roll on top of them.

Chapter 4: Caring for Your Sugar Gliders

What is Your Glider Trying to Say?

As mentioned in previous chapters, gliders make a number of different noises. They are not any more vocal than other house pets, unless they are sick, underfed, lonely, stressed, bored, or aren't comfortable with their owners yet. For all of these reasons it is necessary that you take good care of your sugar gliders. If you do not, they will be sure to let you know with their voices.

As long as they are not bored, stressed, or anything else listed above to make them unsatisfied, your glider will make four primary noises:

Chattering/crabbing

- Surprisingly loud and defensive, sounds like a large insect noise (like a locust).

- They generally stand up on their back legs when making this noise, and may swat at the air.

- Heard during early stages of bonding.

- Means they are a little scared/frightened, a part of their defensive mechanism in the wild to make themselves sound tough.

- Once you have bonded successfully, you should pretty much never hear this sound unless they feel threatened or stressed.

- Don't let this sound intimidate you—you are the boss! Just be gentle and patient with them.

Barking

- Sounds a little like a small dogs bark (like a Chihuahua).

- They generally won't bark without reason, and it could simply mean they are lonely—if you own one sugar glider, and it barks at night, and when you go in to check on it it stops, you may want to consider getting it a little friend, or another trick to try is a night light (night lights are good for groups of sugar gliders that bark as well).

Chirping

- A very soft, gentle, purring sound.

- Generally made while they are feeling affectionate.

Sneezing/hissing

- Could be the sound of a medical infection, but generally it is something else, so don't jump right to that conclusion, just be aware of the possibility.

- Made during their cleaning ritual, since they are very clean little animals.

- They spit on their hands (which is what makes a soft sneezing sound), and then groom their whole body.

- If you notice they are grooming excessively, or continuously cleaning their genitalia, you should consider taking them to the vet for a quick check up in case of infection.

Potty Training

Sugar gliders keep themselves very clean, and they are extremely predictable when it comes to their bathroom habits. However, they cannot be completely trained to use a litter box. Instead, they can be controllable and you can learn how to read their body language when they are out of the cage.

First thing to know is that they do not like to go to the bathroom where they sleep, like most pets. Also, like humans, they go to the bathroom after waking up from a long nap. So, a way to prevent them from have an accident while on your person walking around, in your pocket or in a pouch, you should notice when they wake up and start moving around and provide them with a place to relieve themselves.

There is a process you can go through that will help train the gliders and yourself to help reduce the number of accidents in scenarios like the one provided above. Let's walk through it together:

1. Lay out some newspaper and unscented baby wipes, and set them out in front of the cage before you reach in and pick up your glider.

2. Pick up the baby and stimulate it to go to the bathroom by holding it in one hand and gently wiping its rear end with a cool, moist baby wipe, which will prompt it to begin to relieve itself if it didn't start to go immediately when you picked it up.

3. Let them move from hand to hand, and after a couple minutes this will stimulate them to eliminate anything else that is still in their digestive tract and they will take a couple of seconds or minutes to release a few more droppings or drops of urine.

4. Hold them in one hand again, and repeat the baby wipe technique to allow them to

release anything else they were holding onto, and do this for 30 seconds to a minute to be sure.

This is how you start training a sugar glider to completely relieve itself in a controlled way before you start to handle it during the day, which will make it less likely for large accidents, or any accidents at all. It will take at most 5 minutes total of going through all the above steps to help a trained sugar glider empty itself out when you first take it from the cage.

They generally will not have to go to the bathroom for about 3 hours after this point, unless they have eaten or had something to drink. After they have fallen asleep in your pockets, if you feel one start to wake up and move around, take it out to relieve itself and then give them a snack or a treat.

Keep in mind that in the beginning you will have some accidents, but don't get discouraged and continue the training. Also, every sugar glider has different bathroom habits. Once you get to know each other, potty training and predicting accidents will be easier and easier.

Bonding

If you have gotten your sugar glider from a USDA breeder, be sure to see if they have any good materials on bonding. Generally, breeders will provide you with extensive instructions on the matter, and you should also check to see if they provide ongoing support after purchase.

That being said, here is how you can work on bonding with your baby on your own. As was mentioned previously, the best time for bonding is between 8 and 12 weeks after they have come out of the pouch. You should take them out of their cage and play with them as much as possible. You do not need to wake them up to do this—simply putting them in a bonding pouch or a pocket will do, or letting them exercise in a glider proof room.

They have a sensitive sense of smell, so just having them on your person is a good bonding mechanism. Another way to utilize the sense of smell in bonding is by rubbing small pieces of fleece cloth on yourself, other members of the family, and even other pets, and then leaving the cloth in the nesting box so that when they are sleeping they still smell everyone in your "colony."

They bond in colonies in the wild, and so they do not really need to be only exposed to one human being at a time—feel free to introduce them to other members of the family and other pets (following the steps for introduction to pets mentioned earlier in the book).

When we were talking about sounds, I mentioned the crabbing/chattering sound they make—do not be intimidated by this act! You are the boss and are in charge. Be loving and patient, and don't get scared off just because they are loud and swiping. They cannot do any damage to you.

Here are some things you should keep in mind during the bonding process:

- Use a smaller cage at first (the 2' by 2' by 3' will be fine if you do not feel like building two, but otherwise try an 18" by 18" by 24") so that you can reach in and pick up the glider with no struggle.

- Avoid pulling the baby out of a bonding pouch while it is in its cage—babies and adults love these pouches, but reaching in and invading its space before it has bonded to you will startle and stress it, and perhaps lead it to bite you. Instead, either pull the whole pouch out to attach to yourself when you walk around, or don't use one at all until they have bonded with you, using instead a heat rock and nesting cloth so that they are out in the open but still warm and comfortable.

- If the sugar gliders bite, even after they have bonded to you, they may be trying to tell you they are hungry. You can also try blowing on them, saying "no" in a firm and clear voice, and you might also see that they grow out of it.

- Not all gliders will return to you right away, because they all have different personalities. Some will stay with you, some will go explore and come back on occasion; it really just depends. However, once in your pocket or a bonding pouch on your person during the day, they will be sleepy and generally just curl up and pass right out.

General Care

There are some common questions that people have about sugar gliders that we will try to answer here. One of them is especially important in terms of bonding, which is how to properly hold and handle your sugar glider.

First, never grab them by the tail. Their tails are incredibly sensitive and they need them for flying and balancing, so if they get injured it will be very unfortunate. Hold them gently but firmly—remember that they are very small and delicate. Instead of reaching into their pouches or nests where they are sleeping, just gently roll them out, cupping the baby between your two hands and applying gentle pressure. They like the idea of a tight, dark place because it reminds them of being in their mother's pouch as young. Don't hold too firmly and hurt it, but also don't be so afraid of hurting it that you are too loose with it, which will cause it stress and make it feel insecure.

Handling them in this way during the first couple of days of bonding will help them feel comfortable with you. Eventually, you will find that they fall asleep in your hands in this way. When they feel comfortable enough to do that you can allow them to move around a bit more, and stroke it. Again, don't feel intimidated by any fussing!

You can let them crawl from hand to hand by making a tube of sorts with each hand, and letting them move through one, placing the other hand in front and trading them this way back and forth. They will do this with more confidence as time goes on.

Don't be surprised if handling your glider stimulates it to poop or pee on you. You will avoid this by potty training it and the methods described in that section.

Another topic that doesn't get touched on a lot but is oftentimes perplexing to new parents is how to file a sugar gliders nails. Because they are constantly on you and your clothes and furniture, it is necessary to keep their nails from getting too sharp. But, unlike cats and dogs, you should never just clip the nails. Rather, there is a technique for filing them down so they are manageable.

One of the easiest things to do is to purchase a wheel specifically designed for sugar gliders. The wheels help to naturally file down the nails without you needing to get involved. They have removable inserts that help the process along.

Otherwise, take an ordinary nail file and (after you have bonded and they trust you) have a friend or family member help hold him or her still, and make quick swipes backwards and forwards over the nail tips. Be careful not to go too far because they start to get sensitive, so pay attention as you go to when they start to get very wiggly and you'll know you have done too much. After some practice you will get it right though, don't worry.

How Do You Know If Your Pet Is Sick?

I think it is important to outline some ways you can tell whether or not your sugar glider is getting sick, because they are delicate little creatures and this way you can have some good, concrete symptoms to look out for in case you are feeling nervous, especially as we have talked about stress and loneliness, and as we move soon into the section on glider diet as well.

Generally, gliders are very good at hiding their illness because in the wild sick sugar gliders are often outcast from the colonies so as not to make the colony vulnerable to predators. Here is a list of some things you can be on the lookout for:

- Violent and prolonged shaking or shivering

- Any visible wound

- Dragging of the limbs

- Discharge from the eyes and nose, and particularly wet sneezing sounds

- Swelling or lumps

- Suddenly frantic and uncoordinated movements in climbing and walking, which needs to be monitored because in this state a glider can easily fall and hurt itself from a height

- Change in urine or feces color, consistency, or schedule

- If it has eaten anything that is not food

- If it has fallen into toilet water, which can introduce bacteria or pneumonia

- Changes in weight

- The appearance of not grooming

- Change in the color of the nose, feet, or ears that lasts longer than an hour

- Vomiting

- Changes in body temperature and respiration

- Change in temperament

These are only some of the symptoms to look out for. As I have mentioned throughout this book, you are the best judge of your sugar glider and its behavior, and the better you know it the more you will be able to tell if something is off. Even if it is not listed here, if something unusual is going on and making you nervous, just take it in for a quick check up. As long as you are spending lots of time with it, making sure it has warm places to sit and sleep, and are feeding it a balanced diet, you should have no problems.

Chapter 5: Feeding Your Sugar Gliders

Sugar gliders are omnivores, which means they can eat fruits and vegetables but also some meat. A well-balanced diet will not only keep your sugar glider happy and well nourished, but it will also help it smell better. The Association of Sugar Glider Veterinarians says that 90% of the health problems seen in sugar gliders stem from malnutrition and improper diet.

Many of the homemade diets on the internet are incredibly complicated and make you spend way too much time preparing complex meals that are not really the healthiest possibilities, and aren't any better than the simpler options. Some of these suggestions require you to combine things like eggs, honey, bee pollen, gums, baby foods, supplements, and protein powders—all of these are expensive and some are difficult to find. Also, many people advocate feeding live insects that have been prepared with vitamins and nutrients as well, which is just overkill.

On the other hand, there are many extremely well developed pellet foods, which are inexpensive and have all the necessary nutrients. The ASGV recommends brands called "Glide-R-Chow" and "NutriMax." These pellet brands will make feeding your glider cost around $5 per month.

There are also some nutritional supplements known as "gravy" that you can add on to the pellet feed, and the ASGV recommends "Glide-R-Gravy." The gravy just has all of the stuff that people put in to the fancy homemade diets, but in a convenient and affordable way. If you put a tablespoon of that over their pellets every night before you put them away, they will be good to go, for the most part. You will have handled 75% of their diets.

The next 25% should be fresh fruits and veggies that you have been sure to wash to remove any contaminants from the farm fields and grocery stores. Some websites say that the percentage of fruits and veggies should be higher, but that can actually harm your sugar glider and its digestion because there are too many sugars in fruits and veggies. It is like candy to them, junk food in a way, when they need more of the healthy proteins in the pellets. So, 25% of their daily diet would be about 1/8th a slice of an apple, or equal to that in other fruits or veggies instead, per day and animal.

You should also ensure that they have a healthy serving of calcium. Without these nutrients, the bones of sugar gliders can quickly become delicate and fragile. Phosphorus inhibits the body's ability to absorb calcium, so be sure that when you supplement calcium in their diets try to find one that doesn't contain phosphorus. This is because lots of what you are going to feed your sugar gliders has a high amount of phosphorus, so just be sure to give plenty of calcium to make sure that they get enough.

Corn contains a very high amount of phosphorus, as do alfala sprouts, apples without skin, apricots, beets, nectarines, peas, and yams. Please note that you can still feed these things to your glider, just be aware of the phosphorus and calcium ratio.

Many serious health complications come from lack of mineral and vitamins. All of the pellet foods mentioned earlier have specific types and brands of multivitamins recommended as supplements —if you follow the advice on the labels, you won't risk overdoing one or the other of the vitamins, which could cause problems just as it can in people. If you do not want to use the vitamin recommended by the pellet brand you are using, at least be sure to buy a vitamin that is specifically designed for sugar gliders.

The next most important thing to make sure you keep an eye on is the amount of water available to the sugar glider. Sugar gliders can dehydrate very quickly and die without enough water. Use filtered water. It is common for some people to take a gallon of water and add 1/4 cup of organic apple cider vinegar to it as a natural antibiotic. However, it is possible to overdo the vinegar, so more is definitely not better.

All totaled, these things should only cost about $10 to $15 a month.

Don't feel too overwhelmed by everything—I know the diet sounds a little complicated. But here is how you go about it. I will continue on at the moment as if you are basing the diet off of a pellet and gravy foundation.

- Put about 10 to 15 pellets in the bowl every day, and cover them with 1 to 2 tablespoons of gravy every night. This happens just once a day, and the bulk of the diet is done! See, not so bad after all.

- Then, dice up the fruits and/or vegetables in the cage every night just before you go to sleep, not too small so they don't dry out.

- The last step is to sprinkle the multi-vitamin over the fruits and veggies, and that is it.

- A great treat is a small piece of wheat bread at night in their cage, but don't do it more than a couple of times a week or they will get spoiled and won't eat the rest of their food.

So, you see in the end, it really isn't too complicated to feed a sugar glider once it is all explained step by step. If you notice the food getting thrown around and ending up in the bottom of the cage in the tray a lot, you can try to make them less wasteful by creating a small dining room out of a plastic bowl or box with two holes on either side, and putting the food under there. This will help them eat in a contained way, without playing with their food.

Recipe of Homemade Diet

I will now outline possibilities for creating a homemade diet, if you would prefer to go that route instead. There are many diets online; this is only one option. It is the basic system of something called "Bourbon's Modified Leadbeater's" diet, using the BML mixture listed below and other added ingredients.

Instructions:

- 1/2 cup honey—not honeycomb, raw, or unfiltered honey.

- 1 egg, boiled or scrambled—you can use the shell if you would like, just make sure it is broken into teeny tiny pieces by the blender so the glider doesn't choke.

- 1/4 cup apple juice—not frozen or anything special, just regular bottled apple juice.

- Blend all these ingredients in a blender, then start adding the next ingredients.

- One 4 oz bottle of premixed Gerber juice with yogurt—can be substituted with 2 oz of plain yogurt and 2 oz of mixed fruit juice.

- 1 tsp of rep cal "Herptivite" vitamin supplement—can be ordered through your pet store.

- Blend again.

- 2 tsps rep-cal calcium supplement non-phosophorous with vitamin D-4—also can be ordered through the pet store.

- Two 2-1/2 oz jars of stage 1 or stage 2 Heinz, Gerber, or Beechnut Chicken baby food—either with chicken gravy or chicken broth.

- 1/4 cup wheat germ.

- 1/2 cup dry baby cereal—mixed or oatmeal.

- Blend again, pour into a Tupperware bowl or ice cube trays and freeze it.

Don't mix the fruits and veggies into anything before freezing; they should be fed to the glider fresh. Feed this to your sugar glider by mixing 1 tablespoon of the BML mix, 1 tablespoon of fruits, 1 tablespoon of veggies, and insects. Don't use canned fruits or the pits of fruits.

Please note that this diet recommends a far great ratio of fruits and vegetables than was recommended by the Association of Sugar Glider Veterinarians.

Now, some people also recommend feeding them live crickets and mealworms because this is part of their diet in the wild. This is true, but it is up to you whether or not you want live bugs in the cages to potentially escape through the wire mesh. Also, feeding them live bugs can cause them to smell a little more than otherwise. If anything, live insects should be considered a treat

Treats

I already mentioned wheat bread and insects as occasional treats, but there are a couple of other options as well, and some things to watch out for when giving special treats.

The number one thing to watch out for is feeding them too many, because they will stop wanting the healthy stuff and only want the sweet stuff.

So, as a general rule, treats should only consist of 5% of the daily diet (which is already pretty small, so that's not a lot!). Giving them one entire blackberry for example would be like us sitting down to an entire watermelon at once.

Also, try to avoid giving treats to anyone who has been out of the pouch for less than 15 weeks because their digestive systems are still sensitive, and always introduce new treats slowly to watch out for diarrhea.

Some other examples of good treats for sugar gliders are small dabs of flavored yogurt or applesauce, small pieces of fruits, and small pieces of dehydrated fruits.

Foods to Avoid

Now that we know what foods are good for sugar gliders, let's talk about foods that are dangerous for them. Here is a small list of foods that you should keep away from your gliders:

- Chocolate—even a small amount of chocolate can be fatal.

- Most dairy products, such as ice cream and cheese—sugar gliders are, in general, lactose intolerant, and the most that gliders will usually be able to handle is a small amount of flavored yogurt every once in a while

- Any fruit or vegetable normally treated with pesticides that are difficult to clean thoroughly, like blackberries, broccoli, cauliflower, etc

- Occasionally grapes and raisins can be used as treats

Most importantly, remember that anything in excess can hurt any pet, so just remember that sugar gliders are very small and a little goes a long way. As always, use your best judgment.

Conclusion

Hopefully this book has helped you decide some very important things on your journey to owning a sugar glider, and also provided some useful information. We have discussed some basic sugar glider anatomy, physiology, and habits. We have gone over some things to consider before buying and during the buying or adoption process, and even how to build a cage and create a diet for your little pet, and also of course how to get acquainted with it through the bonding process.

Remember that sugar gliders can live for up to 15 years, so be sure to really consider the first section of this book carefully where we discuss whether or not you are prepared to introduce one into your life. It is a big responsibility, and it would be unfortunate for you to go through all the work for creating space for it and making it comfortable to discover two weeks in that you have made a mistake and weren't actually prepared for one.

Also, always use your best judgment when it comes to caring for your sugar glider, and be aware that many Internet sources do not always offer the best or the most well-intentioned advice. Your breeder is a great source of information, and there are sugar glider owner communities and forums you can contact as well. When in doubt, either find a great book (maybe consider building a small library for your biggest questions and concerns), or call the breeder.

I hope you find great happiness with your new baby. You are in for a friendship based on companionship and affection. When all is said and done, sugar gliders are clean, adorable, friendly, and quiet (during the day, and at night they just move around a lot!). And if you are willing to spend the time with them that they need, it could be a very good relationship. Good luck!

Made in the USA
Monee, IL
29 November 2021